LEARN SPEAK AND WRITE

◆ FRENCH ◆

Editor
Sudhir Khanna

Lotus PRESS

4263/3, Ansari Road,
Darya Ganj, New Delhi - 2

LOTUS PRESS
4263/3, Ansari Road, Darya Ganj, New Delhi-110002
Ph: 32903912, 23280047, E-mail: lotus_press@sify.com
www.lotuspress.co.in

LEARN TO SPEAK AND WRITE FRENCH
© 2005, Lotus Press
ISBN : 81-89093-85-1
Reprint: 2006, 2007

Published by: Lotus Press
Designed and Typeset by: Glow - Worms, New Delhi
Printed at: Gyan Sagar, Delhi

Introduction To The Book...

Our books on **FOREIGN LANGUAGES** have been designed keeping in mind the increasing number of tourists, businessmen and others who visit these countries very often.

These books can also serve as a basis for a more complete study of these languages.

Learners who use these books can easily make themselves understood where these languages are spoken. By reading these books, one is not required to learn a long list of grammatical rules.

The vocabularies in these books have been carefully selected to give every learner the words that are needed in all aspects of everyday life.

We, at Lotus Press, are pretty confident that these books will give the learners a useful introduction to these languages as they are spoken and written. This can eventually lead the learners to achieve a complete mastery on their chosen language.

LEARN TO SPEAK AND WRITE **FRENCH** helps you to get acquainted with the French language. This will surely enable you to speak and write French as fluently just the way the typical French do. Happy learning ...

– Publishers ◆

◆ TABLE OF CONTENTS ◆

The French Alphabet

Alphabet	French Symbol	Pronunciation	Hindi
A, a	a	ah	आ
B, b	bé	bay	बे
C, c	cé	say	से
D, d	dé	day	दे
E, e	ə	uh	अ
F, f	eff	eff	ऐफ़
G, g	ӕ	zhay	ज़े
H, h	ache	ahsh	आश
I, i	i	ee	ई
J, j	ji	zhee	जी
K, k	ka	kah	का
L, l	elle	el	ऐल
M, m	emme	em	ऐम
N, n	enne	en	ऐन

Alphabet	French Symbol	Pronunciation	Hindi
O, o	o	oh	ओ
P, p	pé	pay	पे
Q, q	ku	kew	क्यू
R, r	err	err	ऐर
S, s	esse	ess	ऐस
T, t	té	tay	ते
U, u	u	ew	इयु
V, v	vé	vay	वे
W, w	double vé	doobluhvay	दुब्लवे
X, x	ikss	eeks	ईक्स
Y, y	igrek	eegrek	ईग्रैक
Z, z	zedd	zed	ज़ैद

After reading and going through this French Alphabet, you may find this language little difficult because it is indeed very different from English. But let me assure you that nothing is difficult to learn if your determination is strong enough and you have a proper guidance.

Lesson 1

Pronunciation Guidelines

French language, as any other widely spread language, has many various flavours depending on where it is spoken.

This book is intended to teach you the International French so that you should be understood by any French speaking people wherever you are.

However, you may experience some difficulties for understanding what the person you are talking with is telling you.

The aim of this book is to give you some expressions used in France and outside France to help you in understanding French-speaking people around the *Francophonie* (French-speaking community around the world).

A written course is the best suited means to learn how to pronounce a language, especially when you have never heard it.

In addition, the way people pronounce their own language may tremendously vary from one place to another and is strongly dependent on the local culture, customs and neighbouring influences.

This remark is particularly true for French language: there are startling pronunciation differences between the French spoken in southern France, in northern France, in Belgium, in Switzerland, in Quebec and in the many French speaking African countries (Morocco, Algeria, Tunisia, Senegal, Ivory Coast, Zaire, Burundi, Rwanda, Cameroon, Gabon, Niger, Burkina Faso, Chad, etc.), in such a way that people may not understand each other!

So, you understand that one has to agree on a standard.

Hopefully, such a standard exists and is commonly referred to as "*International French*" also improperly called "*Parisian French*".

The aim of this first lesson is to give you guidelines for the pronunciation of the main French sounds, i.e. single vowels, vowels combinations and the consonants whose pronunciation differs from the English one.

This is not an exhaustive description of the French pronunciation since it does not make any sense to try to cover all aspects of the pronunciation of a language until you can hear the actual sounds.

As mentioned above, learning how to pronounce a language from a written course is not a very tough job.

So, French will be no longer a dark mystery for you !!!

Though English and French share a good bunch of

words, their pronunciation is completely different. Moreover, in French there are some sounds that do not even exist in English.

Let's start with the vowels.

1. Single Vowels

a (आ)

Pronunciation:

Like the first "**a**" in "marmalade" or in "heart", but just a little bit less open.

Examples:

table (table), sac (bag), chat (cat), rat (rat), bagages (luggage), sa (his/her), bras (arm), matin (morning).

Similar sounds: **â** (more open than a)

e (अ)

Pronunciation:

Like the indefinite article "**a**" in English with a sharper sound, or like the second a in "marmalade".

Examples:

cheveu (hair), deux (two), second [segon] (second), oeuvre (work, as in master works), soeur (sister), heure (hour), beurre (butter).

Similar sounds:

"**eu**" and "**oeu**". The latter one is more open than **e** and **eu**.

i (ई)

Pronunciation:

Like the English "**ee**" but shorter.

Examples:

pipe (pipe), minute (minute), courir (to run), midi (midday), nid (nest).

o (ओ)

Pronunciation:

Two Different Sounds:

an open "**o**" more or less as the English "more" and "for"

a closed one like the English "go" and "low".

Most of the times the "**o**" in French is open. It is closed when located at the end of the word. Note that the difference between open and closed "**o**" is not as stressed as it is in English between the words "open" and "control".

Examples:

Open o: botte (boot), grotte (cave), développer (to develop), homme (man)

Closed o: vélo (bicycle), indigo (indigo)

Similar Sounds:

(to a closed o): "**au**", "**eau**", "**ô**". Examples: eau (water), auto (car), contrôle (control).

u (इयु)

Pronunciation:

The French sound for "**u**" does not exist in English. While in most languages "**u**" is pronounced like the u in "bush", in French it differs dramatically. The French "**u**" is exactly the same sound as the German "**ü**". As we're going to see later, the sound "u" as the English "bush" exists in French as well, but it is formed by the vowel combination "**ou**".

Examples:

voiture (car), minute, humain (human).

y (य)

Pronunciation:

Pronounced the same way as a double French "**i**".

Examples:

❖   noyer [noi-ier] (to drown), rayer [rai-ier] (to scratch), loyer [loi-ier] (rent), pays [pai-i] (country).

❖   For pronunciation, refer to "Vowels and Consonants Combinations" on page 16

Notes

In most cases, the final **e** in a word is not pronounced.

Examples:

bouche [bouch'] (mouth), jambe [jamb'] (leg), lampe [lamp'] (lamp).

When followed by a doubled consonant (**l**, **t**, **p**, **r**, **m**, **n**), **e** is pronounced like the English -ay as in "say", "bay", but without the glide towards **i** and more open. In French, this sound is referred to as "**è**" (**e** with a grave accent).

Examples:

pelle [pèl'] (shovel), mettre [mèttr'] (to put), lettre (letter), terre [tèr'] (land).

2. Accentuated Vowels

One of the most striking differences between the French and the English words is the use of accented characters in French.

Almost every vowel - excepting "**y**" - can be accentuated. Some accents change the sound of the vowel, others don't.

The accents (shown in conjunction with the letter e) are:

the grave accent	-	**è**
the acute accent	-	**é**
the circumflex accent	-	**ê**
the diaeresis	-	**ë**

Accents which Change the Vowel Sound

é is pronounced like the English -ay as in "say", "bay", but without the glide towards **i**.

Same thing for **è** and **ê** but with a much more open sound.

Examples:

frère (brother), père (father), mère (mother), événement (event), blé (wheat), bête (beast or stupid), tête (head).

A diaeresis on an "**i**" makes the syllable sound as if there were two syllables.

Examples:

naïf (naïve) is pronounced [na-if] instead of [nèf] (ai is normally pronounced as an è in French).

â is more open than an "**a**".

Example:

mâcher (to chew), pâte (paste)ô is more closed than "o". Example : hôte (host), contrôle (control)

Accents which do not Change the Vowel Sound

In all other situations, the accent does not affect the sound of the vowel i.e. : **à, ë î ù, ü**. So, what's the need for them? The answer is simple : no need !

But French people are reluctant to change the spelling of their language (as English people !) as opposed to

Spanish and German people.

Most of the French accentuated characters have historical origins. For instance, the "^" was used to indicate that in old French, the vowel was followed by an "**s**".

Thus, the modern French words forêt (forest), hâte (haste), hôte (host), pâte (paste) were spelled as follows in old French : forest, haste, hoste, paste.

As you can notice, these were identical as their English counterparts, or, more precisely, these English words directly come from old French.

3. Vowels and Consonants Combinations

ou
Pronunciation:
like the "**u**" in "bush"

Examples:
bouche (mouth), genou (knee), cou (neck)

oi
Pronunciation:
pronounced like the combination "**oa**"

Examples:
oie (goose), doigt [doa] (finger)

au, eau

Pronunciation:

"ô"

Examples:

eau (water), bateau (ship)

ai

Pronunciation:

"ê"

Examples:

maison [mèzone] (house), j'ai [zhay] (I have), lait (milk), mauvais (bad)

eu, oeu

Pronunciation:

"e"

Examples:

feu (fire), bleu (blue)

ui

Pronunciation:

"u-i" (*two sounds*)

Examples:

aujourd'hui (today), fruit (fruit)

er, et

Pronunciation:

"**é**"

Examples:

boucher (butcher), boulanger (baker). Exceptions: hier [ièr'] (yesterday), et (and)

on

Examples:

bon (good)

an

Examples:

an (year)

en

Examples:

vent (wind)

in, ain, ein

Examples:

matin (morning), main (hand), pain (bread)

un

Examples:

chacun (everybody)

4. Consonants

Most of consonants in French are pronounced in a fairly same way as in English, however, there are some exceptions. In the following list, we're only going to review the consonants whose pronunciation differs in French and in English.

General Rule

The following consonants : **d, n, p, r, s, t, x**, are generally not pronounced when located at the end of a word (*note that they are not pronounced but they generally change the sound of the preceding vowels*).

Conversely, all the other consonants (i.e. the following consonants : **c, f, k, l, q, z**. The other consonants like **b, j, g, v, w**, etc. are rarely or never located at the end of a word) are pronounced.

As many good rule, there are lots of exceptions ! In the progression of this course, the pronunciation rule will be indicated when necessary.

Examples :

trois [troi] (three), vent [vawn] (wind), fonds [fon] (fund).

r

The French "**r**" sound is fairly different from the English one. In English, "**r**" is soft, round. In contrary, in French, "**r**" is guttural and must be pronounced like Scottish people do.

j

The French "**j**" is pronounced like the English "**g**".

Examples:

jardin (garden), jour (day).

g

In French, the pronunciation of "**g**" depends on the subsequent character. If followed by "**a**", "**u**", or "**o**", "**g**" is pronounced like the "**g**" in "garden". If followed by "**e**" or "**i**", it is pronounced like the second "**g**" in "language".

Examples:

langage (language), langue (tongue).

gn

The French sound for "**gn**" is very similar to the Spanish "**ñ**" or like the sound "**nié**".

Examples:

gagner [gañé] (to win), mignon [meeñon] (cute).

ch

The French "**ch**" is pronounced like the English "**sh**".

Examples:

chambre [shawmbr] (room), chat (cat), chaussure (shoe).

h

In French, the character "**h**" is not pronounced when located at the beginning of a word.

Examples:

haricot [arico] (bean), homme [om'] (man), hache [ach'] (ax).

s

As in English, most French words add an "**s**" when plural, however, the last "**s**" in a word is never pronounced.

Examples:

Maison and its plural form maisons are pronounced the same way.

There are, however, some exceptions to this rule, for instance, plus (more) is pronounced [plüss].

Notes:

The pronunciation rules which apply to "**s**" and "**ss**" when located within a word, are the same as in English.

When a word begins with an "**s**", the "**s**" is pronounced like "**ss**" (soft "s").

It is actually the same rule as in English.

5. Numbers 1-10

One	:	un
Two	:	deux [*deu*]
Three	:	trois [*troi*]
Four	:	quatre [*catr'*]
Five	:	cinq [*sanc*]
Six	:	six [*seess*]
Seven	:	sept [*sèt'*]
Eight	:	huit [*weet'*]
Nine	:	neuf [*neuf'*] with an open "**e**"
Ten	:	dix [*diss'*]

Lesson 2

Articles and Genders

Let us study Articles and Genders in French.

1. Genders in French

As opposed to English, French words have a gender. French words can have only two genders : masculine or feminine.

Unfortunately, the distribution of the words in the masculine and the feminine genders does not comply to any logical rule.

Therefore, the only way to know the gender of a word is to learn it by heart.

The **gender** is determined by the **article**, either **definite** (the in English) or **indefinite** (a/an in English).

Masculine definite article:

le [leu]

Feminine definite article:

la

Masculine indefinite article:

un [nasal sound which can be derived from the English sound "**un**" as explained in the first lesson].

Feminine indefinite article:

une [ewn']

The genders of the words introduced in the previous lesson are :

la/une table	:	the/a table
le/un sac	:	the/a bag
le/un chat	:	the/a male cat
la/une chatte	:	the/a female cat
le/un bras	:	the/an arm
la/une soeur	:	the/a sister
la/une bouche	:	the/a mouth
la/une jambe	:	the/a leg
la/une lampe	:	the/a lamp
la/une terre	:	the/a land

la/une botte	:	the/a boot
la/une langue	:	the/a tongue
le/un langage	:	the/a language
la/une chambre	:	the/a room
le/un vélo	:	the/a bike
le/un jour	:	the/a day
la/une nuit	:	the/a night
la/une voiture	:	the/a car
le/un pays	:	the/a country
le/un frère	:	the/a brother
le/un père	:	the/a father
la/une mère	:	the/a mother
la/une tête	:	the/a head
la/une maison	:	the/a house
la main	:	the/a hand
le/un pain	:	the/a bread
la/une tasse	:	the/a cup

When a word begins with a vowel, the definite article that precedes the word is contracted whatever the gender is :

une assiette	:	a plate
l'assiette	:	the plate
un oiseau	:	a bird
l'oiseau	:	the bird
un animal	:	an animal

l'animal	:	the animal
une araignée	:	a spider
L'araignée	:	the spider
une auto	:	a car
l'auto	:	the car

Previously, we told you that there were no logical rules to find out the gender of the French words.

Actually, there are some...

Professions

Almost every profession has two genders depending on whether it is a man or a woman who is accomplishing the work.

Examples:

un boulanger	:	a male baker
une boulangère	:	a female baker
un boucher	:	a male butcher
une bouchère	:	a female butcher

The following list gives the masculine and feminine form of some professions:

Driver

| Masculine | : | un conducteur |
| Feminine | : | une conductrice |

Airplane pilot

Masculine	:	un aviateur
Feminine	:	une aviatrice

Engineer

Masculine	:	un ingénieur
Feminine	:	un ingénieur

Teacher

Masculine	:	un professeur
Feminine	:	un professeur

President

Masculine	:	un président
Feminine	:	une présidente

Minister

Masculine	:	un ministre
Feminine	:	un ministre

Worker

Masculine	:	un ouvrier
Feminine	:	une ouvrière

Animals

Like professions, most animals may have both genders (male and female).

As opposed to professions, the way the female form is built does not comply to any general rule and consequently, must be learnt by heart. The following is a list of examples:

Cat

Masculine	:	un chat [sha]
Feminine	:	une chatte [shat']

Dog

Masculine	:	un chien [shi-èn]
Feminine	:	une chienne [shièn']

Lion

Masculine	:	un lion [li-on]
Feminine	:	une lionne [li-on']

Tiger

Masculine	:	un tigre
Feminine	:	une tigresse [tigrès']

Horse

Masculine	:	un cheval
Feminine	:	une jument

Rabbit

| Masculine | : | un lapin |
| Feminine | : | une lapine |

Rat

| Masculine | : | un rat |
| Feminine | : | un rat |

Pig

| Masculine | : | un porc, un cochon |
| Feminine | : | une truie [tru-i] |

Bovine (cow/bull)

| Masculine (bull) | : | un taureau [toro] |
| Feminine (cow) | : | une vache |

Donkey

| Masculine | : | un âne |
| Feminine | : | une ânesse |

As you may have noticed in the previous examples, the feminine form is often derived from the masculine by appending an "**e**" to the word.

This rule is applicable in most cases and leads to a more general one : the feminine form of nouns and adjectives is built by appending an "**e**" to the masculine form of the word.

This rule is general enough that you should learn it.

2. Plural Articles

The plural form of the **definite** and **indefinite** articles is very simple for it does not vary according to the gender:

Definite article	:	les (feminine and masculine)
Indefinite article	:	des (feminine and masculine)

Plural Rule :

In French, the plural form of nouns and adjectives is built by appending an "**s**" (like in English).

However, in many cases, this rule is not applicable and you will be required to learn by heart the irregular form of plural form of these exceptions.

Examples:

Singular	:	le chat
Plural	:	les chats
Singluar	:	la table
Plural	:	les tables
Singluar	:	un chien
Plural	:	des chiens

Singluar	:	une lionne
Plural	:	des lionnes
Singluar	:	un oiseau
Plural	:	des oiseaux

oiseau is one of these exceptions.

3. Some Usual Expressions

merci	:	thank you
s'il vous plaît	:	please
bonjour	:	literally "good day", means good morning, good afternoon
bonsoir	:	good evening
bonne nuit	:	good night
au revoir	:	literally "see you again", means goodbye
pardon	:	sorry
excusez-moi	:	excuse me

Lesson 3

Pronouns and Verbs

Let us study Pronouns and Verbs in French.

The Verb Groups

In English, the **infinite tense** is built by adding " **to** " in front of the verb : to say, to see, to eat, etc.

In French, the **infinite tense** is indicated by appending **-er**, **-ir** or **-re** to the verb.

Examples :

-er

parl**er**	:	to talk
chant**er**	:	to sing
mang**er**	:	to eat
march**er**	:	to walk

all**er**	:	to go
écout**er**	:	to listen to
lav**er**	:	to wash
commenc**er**	:	to begin

-ir

fin**ir**	:	to end
mour**ir**	:	to die
cour**ir**	:	to run
sent**ir**	:	to feel
av**oir**	:	to have
ven**ir**	:	to come
sav**oir**	:	to know
voul**oir**	:	to want

-re

souri**re**	:	to smile
viv**re**	:	to live
boi**re**	:	to drink
entend**re**	:	to hear
êt**re**	:	to be
condui**re**	:	to drive
vend**re**	:	to sell

The verbs ending with **-er** are referred to as " **first group** " verbs, the verbs ending with **-ir** compose the " **second group** " and the verbs with the ending **-re** form the " **third group** ".

It is useful to distribute the verbs between these 3 groups because different conjugation rules apply to each group:

The pronouns

je	:	I
tu	:	you informal form or "tutoiement" in French
il / elle [il/el']	:	he/she it does not exist in French
nous [nou]	:	we
vous [vou]	:	you when talking to more than one person or formal form "vouvoiement" in French
ils / elles [il/el']	:	they

Notes

In French, there is no neuter pronoun (" **it** " in English). That means that things can be either masculine or feminine as we mentioned in the previous lesson,

in English, the 2nd person pronoun is " **you** " whether in singular or plural.

Informally, in French, if you talk to one single person,

you use " **tu** " and if you talk to a group of people, you must use " **vous** ".

In fact, the " **tu** " form (or " **tutoiement** " in French) is commonly used between people of same age, or same social rank.

When talking to an older person or to somebody above you in rank (*for example your boss*), you must, most of the time, employ the " **vous** " form (or " **vouvoiement** " in French).

" **tu** " marks familiarity while " **vous** " marks respect.

When the verb starts with a vowel, you must use **j'** instead of **je**.

Present Tense

In French, there are much more verb tenses than in English.

Hopefully, a large number of them are rarely, or never, used in the spoken language.

The simplest verb tense is the present which is used to describe actions that occur in the present time.

Conjugating verbs in the present tense is very easy in English because the verb does not change, except for the 3rd singular person where a " **s** " is appended.

In French, the present tense conjugation is not so straight forward.

The verbs termination varies according to the person and the verb group and might be altered.

Let's start with the 1st group verbs :

Conjugation of the 1st group verbs

chanter - to sing

- ❖ je chante [shant']
- ❖ tu chantes [shant']
- ❖ il/elle chante [shant']
- ❖ nous chantons [shanton]
- ❖ vous chantez [shanté]
- ❖ ils/elles chantent [shant']

parler - to speak, to talk

- ❖ je parle [parl']
- ❖ tu parles [parl']
- ❖ il/elle parle [parl']
- ❖ nous parlons [parlon]
- ❖ vous parlez [parlé]
- ❖ ils/elles parlent [parl']

écouter - to listen to

- ❖ j'écoute [écout']
- ❖ tu écoutes [écout']
- ❖ il/elle écoute [écout']
- ❖ nous écoutons [écouton]
- ❖ vous écoutez [écouté]
- ❖ ils/elles écoutent [écout']

You can clearly see the conjugation pattern applying to the termination of the 1st group verbs.

1st person singular	:	**-e**
2nd person singular	:	**-es**
3rd person singular	:	**-e**
1st person plural	:	**-ons**
2nd person plural	:	**-ez**
3rd person plural	:	**-ent**

You should be able to conjugate any other 1st group verb.

Let's try " **aller** " : **j'alle, tu alles**, etc.

Unfortunately, it's wrong!!

" **Aller** " is one of the so many irregular verbs.

The conjugation is rather :

❖   je vais [vé]

❖   tu vas [va]

❖   il/elle va

❖   nous allons

❖   vous allez

❖   ils/elles vont [von]

Now you can figure out why people are used to saying that the French language is difficult!

Conjugation of the 2nd group verbs

finir - to finish

- ❖ je finis
- ❖ tu finis
- ❖ il/elle finit
- ❖ nous finissons
- ❖ vous finissez
- ❖ ils/elles finissent

venir - to come

- ❖ je viens
- ❖ tu viens
- ❖ il/elle vient
- ❖ nous venons
- ❖ vous venez
- ❖ ils/elles viennent

vouloir - to want

- ❖ je veux
- ❖ tu veux
- ❖ il/elle veut
- ❖ nous voulons

- vous voulez
- ils/elles veulent

Once again, the conjugation of 2nd group verbs respect some kind of termination pattern, however, less obvious than in the 1st group.

Some of the 2nd group verbs conjugate like "**finir**" (*termination pattern* : **-s, -s, -t, -ssons, -ssez, -ssent**) and others like "**venir**" (*termination pattern* : **-s, -s, -t**, -ons, **-ez, -ent**).

The case of "**vouloir**" is special for it is an irregular verb.

There is no means to find out easily which pattern applies to a given 2nd group verb, excepting learning it by heart.

Conjugation of the 3rd group verbs

boire - to drink
- je bois
- tu bois
- il/elle boit
- nous buvons
- vous buvez
- ils/elles boivent

vendre - to sell

❖   je vends

❖   tu vends

❖   il/elle vend

❖   nous vendons

❖   vous vendez

◆   ils/elles vendent

vivre - to live

❖   je vis

❖   tu vis

❖   il/elle vit

❖   nous vivons

❖   vous vivez

❖   ils/elles vivent

The 3rd group is a real mess since most of the verbs which belong to it are irregular.

Nevertheless, they respect a termination pattern (**-s**, **-s**, **-t**, **-ons**, **-ez**, **-ent**) but are altered.

No general rule can be drawn up.

" **être** " (to be) and " **avoir** " (to have)

As in many European languages, "**être**" (to be) and

"**avoir**" (to have) play a special role in French.

They are also referred to as auxiliaries. French language makes use of only two auxiliary verbs (**être** and **avoir**) while English has many of them (**to have, will, would, shall, should, can, could, must, might, ought to,** *etc.*).

On one hand, "**être**" and "**avoir**" are strongly irregular but on the other hand, they are used very often.

Consequently, their conjugation must be well known. In the present tense their conjugation are :

être - to be
❖ je suis [su-i]
❖ tu es [ê]
❖ il/elle est [ê]
❖ nous sommes [some]
❖ vous êtes [èt']
❖ ils/elles sont [son]

avoir - to have
❖ j'ai [jé]
❖ tu as [a]
❖ il/elle a
❖ nous avons
❖ vous avez
❖ ils/elles ont [on]

Despite the irregular behaviour of these verbs, the conjugation terminations respect, more or less, the pattern we previously noticed.

Note that this remark is applicable to the verb " **aller** " as well.

SOME COLOURS

bleu	:	blue
rouge	:	red
blanc	:	white
noir	:	black
vert	:	green
jaune	:	yellow
rose	:	pink
orange	:	orange
gris	:	grey
marron / brun	:	brown

This lesson is a bit tough but it is worth learning because verbs are a major component in sentences.

Lesson 4

Adjectives and Plural

Let us study Adjectives and Plural in French.

1. Adjectives

In the second lesson we learnt that in French language, nouns have a gender : they can be either masculine or feminine.

Some of them can be both and the feminine form is derived from the masculine by appending a " **e** "

We also learned how the plural affects the nouns, i.e. by appending a " **s** ", most of the times.

To sum up, we can say that the gender and the number (*singular or plural*) affect the noun's termination, by appending either a " **e** " or a " **s** " (*or sometimes something more complex*).

There is an other kind of words in French which change in accordance to the gender and the number :

The Adjectives

Adjectives change according to the gender and the number of the noun which they qualify.

The rules which are drawn here for the nouns are applicable to the adjectives :

Adjectives Concordance Rules

Rule 1

Concordance with the gender

When the noun which an adjective qualifies is feminine, an " **e** " is appended to the adjective, if it does not already end with an " **e** ".

Rule 2

Concordance with the number

When an adjective refers to a noun in the plural form or more than 1 noun, a " **s** " is appended to it, if it does not end with a " **s** ", a" **z** " or a " **x** ".

Rule 3

The rules 1 and 2 are cumulative, i.e. if an adjective qualifies a feminine and plural noun, it takes an " **e** " and a " **s** " at the end.

Rule 4

Masculine is stronger

When an adjective refers to a group of masculine and feminine nouns, only the masculine concordance rule applies.

This rule is also known as "*the masculine wins over the feminine*", which is more manly French grammar rule !

Note : In most cases, the adjectives follow the noun or the group of nouns they refer.

However, this remark is not rigid and you can actually put an adjective before the noun it qualifies but be careful, by doing this, the meaning may get changed.

Examples :

un homme petit	:	a small man
un petit homme	:	a kid
une femme bonne	:	a good woman
une bonne femme	:	a woman with an uncomplimentary meaning
une voiture sale	:	a dirty car
une sale voiture	:	an awful car

Some adjectives are placed before the noun they qualify rather than after.

Examples :

❖ **grand (big, large)**

We Say	:	**une grande voiture**
Which Means	:	a big car
Rather Than	:	une voiture grande

❖ **beau (beautiful, handsome)**

We say	:	**un beau garçon**
Which Means	:	a handsome boy
Rather than	:	un garçon beau

Note that, in these examples, both forms are grammatically correct but French speaking people prefer the first one.

Examples of adjective concordance rules

Original sentence

Il conduit un camion bleu

Which means	:	He drives a blue truck

Let's apply the four rules we mentioned above :

Rule 1

Concordance with the gender

Il conduit une voiture bleue

Rule 2

Concordance with the number

Il conduit des camions bleus

Rule 3

Accumulation of rules 1 and 2

Il conduit des voitures bleues

Rule 4

Masculine wins over feminine

Il conduit un camion et une voiture bleus

2. Some Adjectives

❖　**big or tall**

masculine singular	:	grand
feminine singular	:	grande
masculine plural	:	grands
feminine plural	:	grandes

❖ **small**

masculine singular	:	petit
feminine singular	:	petite
masculine plural	:	petits
feminine plural	:	petites

❖ **beautiful, handsome**

masculine singular	:	beau
feminine singular	:	belle
masculine plural	:	beaux
feminine plural	:	belles

❖ **ugly**

masculine singular	:	laid
feminine singular	:	laide
masculine plural	:	laids
feminine plural	:	laides

❖ **good**

masculine singular	:	bon
feminine singular	:	bonne
masculine plural	:	bons
feminine plural	:	bonnes

❖ **bad**

masculine singular	:	mauvais
feminine singular	:	mauvaise
masculine plural	:	mauvais
feminine plural	:	mauvaises

❖ **high**

masculine singular	:	haut
feminine singular	:	haute
masculine plural	:	hauts
feminine plural	:	hautes

❖ **low**

masculine singular	:	bas
feminine singular	:	basse
masculine plural	:	bas
feminine plural	:	basses

❖ **heavy**

masculine singular	:	lourd
feminine singular	:	lourde
masculine plural	:	lourds
feminine plural	:	lourdes

❖ **light**

masculine singular	:	léger
feminine singular	:	légère
masculine plural	:	légers
feminine plural	:	légères

❖ **clean**

masculine singular	:	propre
feminine singular	:	propre
masculine plural	:	propres
feminine plural	:	propres

❖ **dirty**

masculine singular	:	sale
feminine singular	:	sale
masculine plural	:	sales
feminine plural	:	sales

❖ **long**

masculine singular	:	long
feminine singular	:	longue
masculine plural	:	longs
feminine plural	:	longues

❖ **short**

masculine singular	:	court
feminine singular	:	courte
masculine plural	:	courts
feminine plural	:	courtes

From this list, you can derive the following additional concordance rules which apply most of the time :

❖ When the masculine singular form of the adjective ends with a e, the feminine form is identical to the masculine one (e.g. sale / sale)

❖ When the masculine singular form of the adjective ends with a n, the feminine form is derived by appending a e and by doubling the ending n (e.g. bon / bonne)

❖ When the masculine singular form of the adjective ends with a er, the feminine form ends by ère (e.g. léger / légère)

❖ When the masculine singular form of the adjective ends with a, **eau**, or **au**, the plural form is composed by appending a **x** and the feminine form is built by replacing eau or au by **elle** (e.g. **beau / belle / beaux**)

3. Our First Sentences

Very simple sentences can be built using a subject, an adjective and the verb **être** (to be) such as :

❖ La maison est grande
   The house is big.

❖ La voiture bleue est chère
   The blue car is expensive.

❖ Tu es grand
   You are tall.

❖ Elle est belle
   She is beautiful.

❖ Les garçons et les filles sont grands
   The boys and the girls are tall.

Note that in this example the "**macho**" rule applies because the adjective grand is only in concordance with the noun garçons.

❖ Nous sommes intelligents
   We are smart.

Note that the concordance rules apply to the adjective according to the gender and the number of the subject.

Learn to Speak and Write FRENCH

We advise you to build such sentences using the few
words you have already learnt.

MORE NUMBERS

11	:	onze (onz)
12	:	douze
13	:	treize [trèz']
14	:	quatorze
15	:	quinze
16	:	seize [sèz']
17	:	dix-sept
18	:	dix-huit [dizuit']
19	:	dix-neuf
20	:	vingt [vin]
30	:	trente
40	:	quarante
50	:	cinquante
60	:	soixante [soissant']
70	:	soixante-dix
80	:	quatre-vingts
90	:	quatre-vingt-dix
100	:	cent [sawn]
200	:	deux cents
1,000	:	mille [meel']
10,000	:	dix mille

✖ 54 ✖

Lesson 5

Sentence Structure

Let us study how to create sentences in French. It's time to build sentences. Stand alone words are rarely useful. To express an idea, whether complex or not, you need to combine words in order to build up sentences.

French language distinguishes three basic sentence structures :

❖ **Normal Sentence Structure**

❖ **Negative Sentence Structure**

✳ **Interrogative Sentence Structure**

A typical French sentence is composed of the following elements :

❖ The people who or the thing which does the action
  It is referred to as the subject of the sentence.

❖ The action
  This is the verb.

❖ The people who or the object which is affected by the action

This element is usually called the accusative or **complément d'objet** direct in French grammar.

We're going to adopt the term accusative

(abbreviation : **ACC**).

❖ The circumstances under which the action takes place (the time, the location, etc.) :

This element is known as the **complément circonstanciel** in French.

We're going to call it circumstances

(abbreviation : **CIR**)

These elements play the role of elementary bricks that compose a sentence.

French, as English, is a positional language, i.e. the function played by words in the sentence depends on their position in the sentence.

So, each kind of sentence is built according to a specific structure or framework.

These structures are very useful because they indicate the position of the various elements (various bricks) in a given kind of sentence (**normal**, **negative** or **interrogative**).

In the context of spoken language they work pretty well. Written language is often more sophisticated than spoken language and leads to more complicated sentences.

Before reviewing the various sentence structures in the present tense, let's learn some prepositions.

1. Some Prepositions

dans	:	in
à	:	to, at
de	:	from, of
sur	:	on

Examples :

❖   Je vis dans une grande ville
    I live in a big city.

❖   Les enfants vont à l'école
    The children are going to school.

❖   Il vient de France
    He comes from France.

❖   Nous marchons sur la route
    We are walking on the road.

2. Normal Sentences

The basic framework of a normal sentence is :

SUBJECT + VERB + ACC + CIR

This structure is comparable to the English one. Examples :

Subject	Verb	ACC	CIR
Tu	chantes	une chanson	dans la rue

Meaning

You sing a song in the street.

Subject	Verb	ACC	CIR
Il	conduit	la voiture	tous les jours

Meaning

He drives the car every day.

Subject	Verb	ACC	CIR
Le boulanger	vend	le pain dans la boulangerie	

Meaning

The baker sells bread in the bakery.

3. Negative Sentences

The basic framework of a negative sentence is :

SUBJECT + ne + VERB + pas + ACC + CIR

The words **ne** ... **pas** play a role similar to (**do not**) in English.

While **do not** is located before the verb, in French the verb is put in between **ne** and **pas**.

Excepting this difference, the structure of a French negative sentence is similar to its English counterpart.

Examples:

❖   Tu ne chantes pas une chanson dans la rue.

❖   Il ne conduit pas la voiture tous les jours.

❖   Le boulanger ne vend pas le pain dans la boulangerie.

Subject	Verb	ACC	CIR
Tu	ne chantes pas	une chanson dans	la rue

Meaning

You do not sing a song in the street.

Subject	Verb	ACC	CIR
Il	ne conduit pas	la voiture	tous les jours

Meaning

He does not drive the car every day.

Subject	Verb	ACC	CIR
Le boulanger	ne vend pas	le pain	dans la boulangerie

Meaning

The baker does not sell bread in the bakery.

4. Interrogative Sentences

The primary goal of interrogative sentences is to ask questions !!

That's what we call in French **"la palissade"** or **"un truisme"** (*something obvious*).

When asking a question, you may want to know

who (*qui in French*) or

what (*que in French*) is performing the action,

when (*quand in French*) the action is performed,

how (*comment in French*) or

where (*où in French*) it is performed, etc.

Most of questions need an interrogative conjunction which indicates what we want to know. The basic interrogative conjunctions are :

qui	:	who
que	:	what
pourquoi	:	why

comment	:	how
quand	:	when
où	:	where
combien	:	how many, how much

Compared to the normal and negative structures, the interrogative sentences are a little bit more complicated.

Basically, French language provides two interrogative structures :

❖ **A spoken language oriented structure**

❖ **A written language oriented one**

As the spoken language is always simpler than the written one, the first structure is easier to understand. So, let's start with it.

The basic structure is :

Interrogative conjunction + est-ce que + SUBJECT + VERB + ACC + CIR + ?

Once again, the group of words **est-ce que** plays a role similar to (**do**) in the English interrogative sentences.

As we see, the structure of a French interrogative sentence is similar to its English counterpart.

Note that the interrogative conjunction is optional depending on what you want to know.

Examples :

Question

Est-ce que tu chantes une chanson dans la rue ?

Do you sing a song in the street ?

Answer

oui (*yes*) or non (*no*).

Question

Qu'est-ce que tu chantes dans la rue ?

What do you sing in the street ?

Answer

Je chante une chanson.

I sing a song.

Question

Est-ce qu'il conduit la voiture tous les jours ?

Does he drive the car every day ?

Answer

Oui, il conduit la voiture tous les jours.

Yes, he drives the car every day.

Question

Quand est-ce qu'il conduit la voiture ?

When does he drive the car ?

Answer

Il conduit la voiture tous les jours.

He drives the car every day.

Question

Est-ce que le boulanger vend le pain dans la boulangerie?

Does the baker sell the bread in the bakery ?

Answer

Oui (*yes*) or non (*no*).

Question

Qui est-ce qui vend le pain dans la boulangerie ?

Who sells the bread in the bakery ?

Answer

Le boulanger.

The baker.

Question

Combien de frères as-tu ?

How many brothers do you have ?

Answer

J'ai deux frères.

I have two brothers or simply : **Deux** *(two).*

Notes :

❖   When **que** is followed by a word starting with a vowel, **que** is contracted to **qu'**. This rule is illustrated in the examples **Qu'est-ce qu'il** and **Est-ce qu'il** and is general.

We have already mentioned the same kind of contraction with the pronoun **je** (I) : **je mange** (I eat) and **j'achète** (I buy).

❖   When used with the conjunction **qui** (who) , **est-ce que** is replaced by **est-ce qui** resulting in **Qui est-ce qui**.

This alteration is not a caprice of the French language but is conversely governed by strict grammatical rules.

The **que** and the **qui** we are talking about here belong to the pronouns category, as we are going to see later in this course.

❖   **Est-ce que** does not depend on the gender nor the number of the subject while the English (**do**) must respect the conjugation pattern of to do.

For the first time, French is simpler than English

❖   In French, when you answer a question by only **oui** (yes) or **non** (no) you are not required to repeat the subject and the verb as in English (yes I do, no we don't, yes she does, etc.). However, it is not grammatically incorrect to repeat the subject. You may want to do that in order to emphasize your answer. If you do so, you have to repeat all the words of the question.

Examples:

Oui, je chante une chanson

Yes, I do sing a song.

Non, il ne conduit pas la voiture tous les jours

No, he does not drive the car every day.

Now, we can introduce the second interrogative structure.

Basically, this structure consists of switching the position of the subject and the verb like this:

Interrogative conjunction + VERB + - + SUBJECT + ACC + CIR + ?

Again, the interrogative conjunction is not mandatory.

Examples :

Questions	Answers
Chantes-tu une chanson dans la rue ?	oui or non
Où chantes-tu une chanson ?	Dans la rue
Que chantes-tu dans la rue ?	Une chanson
Conduit-il la voiture tous les jours ?	oui or non
Que conduit-il tous les jours ?	La voiture
Quand conduit-il la voiture ?	Tous les jours

However, the pattern only applies when the subject is a pronoun (**je, tu, il/elle, nous, vous, ils/elles**).

Otherwise, it is not so straight forward.

When the subject is not a pronoun, the interrogative structure is :

Interrogative conjunction + SUBJECT + VERB + - + PRONOUN + ACC + CIR + ?

The pronoun which is added must be in accordance with the gender and the number of the subject.

Examples :

Normal sentence :

Le boulanger vend le pain dans la boulangerie.

Interrogative Sentences

1. Le boulanger vend-il le pain dans la boulangerie ?

2. Où le boulanger vend-il le pain ?

3. Que le boulanger vend-il ?

Explanations : "Le boulanger" is masculine singular.

The corresponding pronoun is "il"

Normal Sentence

La boulangère vend le pain dans la boulangerie.

Interrogative Sentences :

1. La boulangère vend-elle le pain dans la boulangerie ?

2. Où la boulangère vend-elle le pain ?

3. Que la boulangère vend-elle ?

Explanations : "La boulangère" is feminine and singular. The corresponding pronoun is "elle".

Normal Sentence

Les boulangères vendent le pain dans la boulangerie.

Interrogative Sentences

1. Les boulangères vendent-elles le pain dans la boulangerie ?

2. Où les boulangères vendent-elles le pain ?

3. Que les boulangères vendent-elles ?

Explanations : "Les boulangères" is feminine and plural. The corresponding pronoun is "elles"

Normal Sentence

Le boulanger et la boulangère vendent le pain dans la boulangerie.

Interrogative Sentences :

1. Le boulanger et la boulangère vendent-ils le pain dans la boulangerie ?

2. Où le boulanger et la boulangère vendent-ils le pain ?

3. Que le boulanger et la boulangère vendent-ils ?

Explanations : "Le boulanger et la boulangère" is a subject which comprises two people, therefore it is plural.

As far as the gender is concerned, you have to remember the macho rule " the masculine wins over the feminine ". Consequently the gender of this subject is masculine.

The corresponding pronoun is then "ils"

This fifth lesson ends the grammatical core of the course. In the next lessons, we're going to focus on the **voca**bulary and the language by itself *i.e.* usual **express**ions, familiar expressions and idiomatic expressions.

Other major verb tenses (past, future and conditional) will be introduced at a steady pace. So carefully go through the next lessons.

5. Exercises

Build up the negative and interrogative sentences for the following normal sentences as shown in the example below :

Normal Sentence :

Pierre chante une chanson dans la rue

Pierre is singing a song in the street.

Negative Sentence :

Pierre ne chante pas une chason dans la rue

Pierre is not singing a song in the street.

Interrogative Sentence #1 :

Où Pierre chante t-il une chanson ?

Answer

dans la rue

Interrogative Sentence #2 :

Que chante Pierre dans la rue ?

Answer

une chanson

Interrogative Sentence #3 :

Qui chante une chanson dans la rue ?

Answer

Pierre

List of Normal Sentences :

❖   Nous conduisons une voiture dans la ville
     We're driving a car in the city.

❖   Monsieur et Madame Dupont habitent une
     maison à Toulouse
     Mr. and Mrs Dupont live in a house in Toulouse.

❖   Elle achète un gâteau dans la pâtisserie
     She buys a cake in the cake shop.

❖   Les enfants jouent au football dans le jardin
     The children play soccer in the garden.

Lesson 6

The Family

Let's learn some more French vocabulary.

Nouns

le père	:	the father
la mère	:	the mother
papa	:	daddy
maman	:	mummy
le frère	:	the brother
la soeur	:	the sister
le fils [fiss]	:	the son
la fille	:	the daughter, the girl
le garçon	:	the boy
un enfant	:	a child
les enfants	:	the children
Monsieur	:	Mr.
abréviation M.	:	*abbreviation M.*

Madame	:	Mrs.
abréviation Mme.	:	abbreviation Mme.
la famille	:	the family
nom	:	name, last name, surname
prénom	:	first name, given name
âge	:	age

Verbs

| appeler | : | to call |
| habiter | : | to live |

Conversation

Following is a short text describing the Dupont family.

Monsieur et Madame Dupont ont deux enfants
Mr. and Mrs. Dupont have two children.

Ils ont un garçon et une fille
They have a boy and a girl.

Le garçon s'appelle Pierre
The boy is called Pierre.

La soeur de Pierre s'appelle Caroline
Pierre's sister is called Caroline.

Conversation

L'institutrice : Comment t'appelles-tu ?
The teacher : What's your name?

Pierre : Je m' appelle Pierre.
Pierre : My name is Pierre.

L'institutrice : Quel âge as-tu ?
The teacher : How old are you ?

Pierre : J'ai dix ans.
Pierre : I am ten.

L'institutrice : Est-ce que tu as des frères et soeurs ?
The teacher : Do you have any brother or sister ?

Pierre : Oui. J'ai une soeur.
Pierre : Yes, I have one sister.

L'institutrice : Quel âge a-t-elle ?
The teacher : How old is she ?

Pierre : Elle a huit ans.
Piere : She is eight.

L'institutrice : Quel est ton nom de famille ?
The teacher : What's your surname ?

Pierre : Dupont
Pierre : Dupont.

L'institutrice : Où est-ce que tu habites ?
The teacher : Where do you live ?

Pierre : J'habite à Toulouse.
Pierre : I live in Toulouse.

Notes on Pronunciation

One of the major characteristics of French pronunciation is the usage of what we call in French **liaisons**.

Liaisons are links between words. As mentioned in the first lesson (*Guidelines for French Pronunciation*), most of the time, the final character of a word is not pronounced.

This rule is generally true but its scope is limited to separate words. When words are assembled in a sentence, this rule is no longer applicable. Consider two words, for instance **trois** (three) **and enfant** (child).

When put side by side (**trois enfants**), both words are pronounced as if they were linked together to only one word like this **trois_enfants** [*troizawnfawn*].

That's what we call a liaison. In the next lessons, liaisons will be indicated by an **underscore** "_", but keep in mind that the words linked by a liaison are two separate words.

You cannot use liaison between all words. A liaison takes place only when the first word terminates with a consonant and when the second word begins with a vowel.

For example there is no liaison between **trois** (*three*) and **voiture** (*car*).

In addition, some consonants do not sound in a normal way when pronounced in a liaison.

d sounds as **t**

e.g. **grand_enfant** [grawntawnfawn] - tall child,

x sounds as **z**

e.g. **deux_enfants** [deuzawnfawn] - two children,

Unfortunately, as any good rule, the liaison rules have lots of exceptions. In particular, some liaisons don't sound good or sound very weird to a French ear and must be avoided.

No logic can help non French speaking people know whether a liaison must or must not be done. It's better to rely on the indications which are added in the further lessons, as mentioned above (underscore character).

The consonant combination **ll** is very frequent in French. The way you have to pronounce it depends on the character that precedes "**ll**" :

❖   When preceded by a **i** , "**ll**" is pronounced the same way as in Spanish, *i.e.* like a "**y**".

❖   When preceded by a **e**, "**ll**" is pronounced like a "**l**" but changes the sound of the "**e**" to "**è**".

❖   when preceded by any other vowel (i.e. **a, o, u**), "**ll**" is pronounced like a single "**l**".

Let's apply this rule to some words introduced in this lesson :

famille [famiye]	:	family
fille [fiye]	:	daughter, girl
je m'appelle [apèl']	:	I am called
elle [èl']	:	she
balle [bal']	:	ball

When you went through the conversation given before you may have noticed a new strange and weird character : **ç**. "**ç**" is called **c cédille [sé sédiye]** and is pronounced like two "**s**".

Therefore **garçon** is pronounced [**garsson**].

Some other usual words have a **ç** like : **ça** (*this*),

The word **fils** (*son*) is pronounced as if the "**l**" was absent [**fiss**].

Notes on Vocabulary

French people have a **prénom** and a **nom**. The **prénom** is the first name or given name while the nom is the last name or surname.

Pierre's **prénom** is Pierre.

His nom is **Dupont**.

The surname is also referred to as **nom de famille** (*family name*).

To express the age of people, French people don't use the verb **être** (*to be*) as English people do but the verb **avoir** (*to have*) instead.

Thus, we say :

J'ai vingt ans	:	I am twenty
Tu as vingt ans	:	you are twenty
Il/elle a vingt ans	:	He/she/it is twenty
Nous avons vingt ans	:	We are twenty
Vous avez vingt ans	:	You are twenty
Ils/elles ont vingt ans	:	They are twenty

Note that in French, one asks the age of people using the following form :

quel âge as-tu ?

What age do you have ?

Grammar

The conversation given at the beginning of the lesson illustrates two grammatical points :

the usage of the genitive pronouns

the usage of the possessive adjectives

Genitive Pronouns

Genitive is the grammatical name of something very simple. Genitive denotes the ownership.

In English the ownership is indicated by adding **'s** to the owner when it is a human being, or by using **of** when the owner is a thing.

For example :

Mr Dupont has two children, Pierre and Caroline. We can say that Pierre and Caroline are Mr Dupont's children.

When talking about the wheels which belong to a car we say : the wheels of the car (and not the car's wheels).

In English, **'s** and **of** are used to denote the genitive form.

In French, the genitive form is indicated by **de** in the same way as the English **of**.

For instance :

Monsieur Dupont a deux enfants, Pierre et Caroline.

Mr Dupont has two children, Pierre and Caroline.

Pierre et Caroline sont les enfants de Monsieur Dupont

Pierre and Caroline are Mr Dupont's children.

Les roues de la voiture

The wheels of the car.

In French, de is used to express ownership for either persons and things (or animals).

Possessive Adjectives

In English possessive adjectives are : **my**, **your**, **his/her/its**, **our**, **your**, **their**.

Their French counterpart are more complex because they depend on the gender and the number of the object owned by the owner.

For example, when I talk about my bicycle (**vélo** in French) I say **mon vélo** because **vélo** is a masculine singular noun.

When talking about my car (**voiture** in French)   I say **ma voiture** because **voiture** is a feminine singular noun.

When talking about my shoes (**chaussures** in French) I say **mes chaussures** because **chaussures** is a plural noun.

The following table shows how the possessive adjectives vary according to the gender and the number.

Note that when plural, the possessive adjectives is the same whatever the gender.

Possessive Adjectives	Masculine Singular	Feminine Singular	Plural
my	mon	ma	mes
your	ton	ta	tes
his/her/its	son	sa	ses
our	notre	notre	nos
your	votre	votre	vos
their	leur	leur	leurs

Note that as opposed to English, the French possessive adjectives don't depend on the gender of the owner.

Consider Mr and Mrs Dupont's car. Both Mr and Mrs Dupont say, when talking about their car : **ma voiture** .

In addition, let's review the sentences structure. The above conversation contains two kinds of sentence structure : normal and interrogative.

Normal Sentence :

Monsieur et Madame Dupont ont deux enfants. The components are :

the subject (Monsieur et Madame Dupont),

the verb (ont) and

the accusative or complément d'objet direct, thus following the general pattern :

SUBJECT + VERB + ACCUSATIVE

Interrogative Sentence :

Où est-ce que tu habites ?

Where the subject is "**tu**", the verb is "**habites**" and the interrogative conjunction is "**où**".

The sentence pattern is **CONJUNCTION** + **est-ce que** + **VERB** + **SUBJECT ?**

Note that the teacher could have used the other interrogative sentence pattern : **Où habites-tu ?** (**CONJUNCTION** + **VERB** + **SUBJECT**).

Liaisons Guidelines

Monsieur et Madame Dupont ont deux_enfants

Ils_ont un garçon et une fille

Le garçon s'appelle Pierre

La soeur de Pierre s'appelle Caroline

L'institutrice : Comment t'appelles-tu ?

Pierre : Je m'appelle Pierre

L'institutrice : Quel_âge as-tu ?

Pierre : J'ai dix_ans

L'institutrice : Est-ce que tu as des frères et soeurs ?

Pierre : Oui. J'ai une soeur.

L'institutrice : Quel_âge a-t-elle ?

Lesson 7

Where Do You Come From?

Let us learn some more aspects of French.

1. Vocabulary

Noms	:	Nouns
ici	:	here
là	:	there
un pays	:	country
une ville	:	city, town
la citoyenneté	:	citizenship
une destination	:	destination
une origine	:	origin
Verbes	:	**Verbs**
venir	:	to come
aller	:	to go

aller à	:	to go to
venir de	:	to come from
voyager	:	to travel
être né	:	to be born

Adjectifs	:	**Adjectives**
loin	:	far
près	:	close

Prépositions	:	**Prepositions**
de	:	from
à	:	to

Conjonctions	:	**Conjunctions**
quel/quelle/quels	:	what

2. Conversation

La famille Dupont a de nouveaux voisins. Pierre rencontre le fils de ses voisins.

The Dupont Family has new neighbours. Pierre meets the son of his neighbours.

Pierre : Bonjour. Je m'appelle Pierre. Comment t'appelles-tu ?

Pierre : Hello, my name is Pierre. What is your name ?

Peter : Je m'appelle Peter

Peter : My name is Peter.

Pierre : D'où est-ce que tu viens ?

Pierre : Where do you come from ?

Peter : Je viens d'Angleterre. Mes parents sont anglais.

Peter : I come from England. My parents are English.

Pierre : Super ! Est-ce que tu viens de Londres ?

Pierre : Wonderful ! Do you come from London ?

Peter : Oui. Je suis né à Londres.

Peter : Yes. I was born in London.

Pierre : Tu parles bien français. Moi, je ne parle pas anglais.

Pierre : You speak French well. As far as I am concerned, I don't speak English.

3. Notes on Vocabulary

Countries and Citizenship

In French, as in English, the first character of country names must be uppercase, while the uppercase is not required for the citizenship.

Example (refer to the " additional vocabulary " section for more country names) :

Country	Citizenship
France	français (French)
Belgique (Belgium)	belge (Belgian)
Suisse (Switzerland)	suisse (Swiss)
Angleterre (England)	anglais (English)
Allemagne (Germany)	allemand (German)
Italie (Italy)	italien (Italian)
Espagne (Spain)	espagnol (Spanish)
Irlande (Ireland)	irlandais (Irish)
Russie (Russia)	russe (Russian)
États Unis d'Amérique (USA)	américain (American)
Canada (Canada)	canadien (Canadian)
Québec (Quebec)	québécois (Quebecer)
Chine (China)	chinois (Chinese)
Japon (Japan)	japonnais (Japanese)

Note that, as opposed to English, the citizenship cannot be easily derived from the country name.

Citizenship is similar to an adjective [**je suis français** (*I am French*)].

Consequently, citizenship must be in accordance with the gender and the number of the people considered.

Example :

Elle est anglaise	:	She is English
Mes amis sont américains	:	My friends are American
Les chinois et les chinoises ne sont pas grands	:	Chinese men and women are not tall

As same as citizenship, the way French people call the inhabitants of a city is not straight forward.

The list below provides some examples:

City	:	Inhabitant
Paris	:	parisien
Marseille	:	marseillais
Lyon	:	lyonnais
Lille	:	lillois
Toulouse	:	toulousain
Bruxelles	:	bruxellois
Geneve (Geneva)	:	genèvois
Rome	:	romain
Londres (London)	:	londonien
Berlin	:	berlinois

New York	:	new-yorkais
Pékin (Beijing)	:	pékinois

There are some striking irregular examples :

City	:	**Inhabitant**
Saint Étienne	:	stéphanois
Saint Malo	:	malouin
Bordeaux	:	bordelais
Madrid	:	madrilène
Moscou	:	moscovite

Prepositions de and à

When used with verbs expressing a movement, the preposition **de** means from, while **à** means to.

Therefore, they are both key prepositions in French language.

Examples:

venir de	:	to come from
aller à	:	to go to

More precisely, **de** and **à** refer to locations and not to movements. **de** refers to the origin of the movement and **à** refers to the destination.

To illustrate that, consider the following expression :

d'ici à là [**d'ici** is the contraction of **de ici**] which means from here to there (**ici** = here, **là** = there).

Note that **de** and **à** have both different meanings depending on the verb they are associated with or their role in the sentence.

For instance, we have already mentioned that **de** is used to express the genitive relationship between two words.

4. Liaisons Guidelines

Pierre : Bonjour. Je m'appelle Pierre.

       Comment t'appelles-tu ?

Peter : Je m'appelle Peter

Pierre : D'où est-ce que tu viens ?

Peter : Je viens d'Angleterre.

       Mes parents sont anglais.

Pierre : Super ! Est-ce que tu viens de Londres ?

Peter : Oui. Je suis né à Londres.

Pierre : Tu parles bien français.

       Moi, je ne parle pas_anglais.

Lesson 8

Comparing

Let us learn some more French Vocabulary, Conversational Skills, Grammar, Liaison Guidelines and Ordinal Numbers.

1. Vocabulary

Noms	:	Nouns
un collègue	:	a colleague
un travail	:	a job, a work
un restaurant	:	a restaurant
une voiture	:	a car
une idée	:	an idea
un litre	:	a liter
un kilomètre	:	a kilometer
un mètre	:	a meter
un mètre carré	:	a square meter

un mètre cube	:	a cubic meter
une garantie	:	a warranty

Verbes	:	**Verbs**
rencontrer	:	to meet
acheter	:	to buy
vendre	:	to sell
coûter	:	to cost
changer	:	to change
devoir	:	must, to have to
aimer	:	to like, to love
trouver	:	to find
consommer	:	to consume
vouloir	:	to want
avoir raison	:	to be right
avoir tort	:	to be wrong

Adjectifs (Adjectives)

❖ nouveau (m.s.), nouvelle (f.s.), nouveaux (m.p) (***new***)

❖ vieux (m), vieille (f) (***old***)

❖ superbe (***superb***)

❖ cher (m), chère (f) (***expensive***)

❖ bon marché (***cheap***)

❖ beau (m), belle (f), beaux (m.p.) (***beautiful***)

❖ actuel (m), actuelle (f) (***current, present***)

❖   puissant (m), puissante (f) (***powerful***)

❖   *performant* (m), *performante* (f) (***efficient***)

Conjonctions	:	Conjunctions
pourquoi	:	why
parce que	:	because
combien	:	how much, how many
trop + adjectif	:	too + adjective
beaucoup	:	much

2. Conversation

Monsieur Dupont rencontre un collègue de travail au restaurant.

Mister Dupont meets a colleague in a restaurant.

M. Dupont : J'ai envie d'acheter une nouvelle voiture.

M. Dupont : I'd like to buy a new car.

Le collègue : Pourquoi ?

The colleague : Why ?

M. Dupont : Parce que ma voiture est trop vieille. Je dois la changer.

M. Dupont : Because my car is too old. I must replace it.

Le collègue : Est-ce que tu as une idée de ce que tu veux acheter ?

The colleague : Do you have an idea of what you want to buy ?

M. Dupont : Oui. J'aimerais acheter la nouvelle Renault. Elle est superbe.

M. Dupont : Yes. I'd like to buy the new Renault. It is superb.

Le collègue : Oui, mais elle doit coûter cher, n'est-ce pas?

The colleague : Yes but it must be expensive, isn't it ?

M. Dupont : En effet, elle coûte cher, mais elle est moins cher que la nouvelle Peugeot. C'est la plus performante et elle a la meilleure garantie.

M. Dupont : Indeed it is expensive but is less expensive than the new Peugeot. It is the most efficient and it has the best warranty.

Le collègue : Combien consomme-t-elle ?

The colleague : How much gas does it consume ?

M. Dupont : Sept litres au cent. Ce n'est pas beaucoup. C'est beaucoup moins que ma voiture actuelle. En plus, elle est plus puissante.

M. Dupont : Seven litres every one hundred kilometers. It is not much. It is far less than my current car. In addition, it is more powerful.

Le collègue : Tu as raison. Tu fais une bonne affaire.

The colleague : You're right. You are making a good deal.

3. Notes on Vocabulary

To be right / to be wrong

The French counterparts of the English to be right and to be wrong are **avoir raison** and **avoir tort**. While in English one uses the verb to be in French one uses **avoir** (*to have*).

Emphasizing Questions

Consider the following question : Is this car expensive ? You ask this question because you don't have any idea of the price of the car being considered. You expect that the person we are talking to tells you the price of the car. Now, imagine you already know the price of the car, and it is really expensive. You surely don't ask your question the same way. You would probably say : This car is expensive. Isn't it ?

In French it is possible to emphasize your questions the same way. The normal interrogative form is : **Est-ce que cette voiture est chère ?** But, if you already know that it is expensive and emphasize the fact that it is expensive you could say : **Cette voiture est chère. N'est-ce pas ?** In the latter sentence, **n'est-ce pas** plays exactly the same role as the English isn't it. There is, however, a difference between the English and the French form.

It is ...

The expression (**it is**) is translated in French by **Cela est** or more currently by the contracted form **C'est**.

To some extent, **cela** or **c'** plays a similar role as it. However, **cela** must not be considered as the impersonal pronoun.

There is no impersonal pronoun in French (it in English) because things and animals are either masculine or feminine.

Examples :

❖ C'est une belle voiturre (*It is a beautiful car*)

❖ C'est une grande maison (*It is a big house*)

❖ C'est un homme agréable (*He is a pleasant man. Literally : It is a pleasant man*).

4. Grammar

Comparative and Superlative Forms

Comparatives are used to compare things. A comparison can express a superiority, an inferiority or an equality relationship. In English the comparisons are expressed as follows :

Superiority

My car is more performing than yours.

My car is nicer than yours.

Inferiority

Your car is less performing than mine.

Your car is less nice than mine.

Equality

Your car is as performing as mine.

My car is as nice as yours.

In French, there is only one superiority comparison form built as follows, regardless of the length of the adjective :

Plus + Adjective + Que

As we can notice, plus is equivalent to more, and que is equivalent to than.

Examples :

Ma voiture est plus performante que la tienne.

Ma voiture est plus belle que la tienne.

The inferiority form is composed like this :

Moins + Adjective + Que

where **moins** plays the same role as **less** and **que** the same role as than.

Examples :

Ta voiture est moins performante que la mienne.

Ta voiture est moins belle que la mienne.

The equality comparison is formed as follows :

Aussi + Adjective + Que

where **aussi** plays the same role as **as** and **que** the same role as **as**.

Examples :

Ma voiture est aussi performante que la tienne.

Ta voiture est aussi belle que la mienne.

Note that, the adjective must respect the concordance rules with the gender and the number.

Superlatives are used to denote the highest degree of an adjective (*or an adverb*).

In English, superlatives are built up by appending an adjective with the termination **-est** or by adding most before.

In French, the superlative form of an adjective is derived by adding plus before.

Note that plus plays a similar role as most in English. However, while in English, the superlative is preceded by the definite article the, in French, the definite article must be in accordance with the gender and the number of the noun(s) it refers to.

Examples :

Ma voiture est la plus performante.

Ma voiture est la plus belle.

Examples :

Ta voiture est la moins performante.

Ma voiture est la moins belle.

These rules are very simple and apply to almost every adjective. Unfortunately there are a few exceptions, as in English !

bon (good)

❖   superiority comparative : meilleur que

❖   inferiority comparative : moins bon / bonne que

❖   equality comparative : aussi bon / bonne que

❖   superiority superlative : le / la meilleur / meilleure

❖   inferiority superlative : le / la moins bon / bonne

mauvais (bad)

❖   superiority comparative : pire que or plus mauvais que (both are correct)

❖   inferiority comparative : moins mauvais / mauvaise que

❖   equality comparative : aussi mauvais / mauvaise que

❖ superiority superlative : le/la pire or le/la plus mauvais/mauvaise

❖ inferiority superlative : le/la moins mauvais/mauvaise

Expressing a wish

In French, people express a wish by using the conditional tense. It is pretty the same as in English.

The conditional present conjugation for **aimer** (*to like*) and **vouloir** (*to want*) is listed below.

Aimer

❖ J'aimerais
❖ Tu aimerais
❖ Il/elle aimerait
❖ Nous aimerions
❖ Vous aimeriez
❖ Ils/elles aimeraient

Vouloir

❖ Je voudrais
❖ Tu voudrais
❖ Il/elle voudrait
❖ Nous voudrions
❖ Vous voudriez

❖   Ils/elles voudraient

Conjugation Pattern :

❖   -ais
❖   -ais
❖   -ait
❖   -ions
❖   -iez
❖   -aient

Irregular Conjugation

Vouloir (to want)

❖   Je veux
❖   Tu veux
❖   Il/elle veut
❖   Nous voulons
❖   Vous voulez
❖   Ils/elles veulent

Devoir (must)

❖   Je dois
❖   Tu dois
❖   Il/elle doit
❖   Nous devons
❖   Vous devez
❖   Ils/elles doivent

Vendre (to sell)

❖ Je vends

❖ Tu vends

❖ Il/elle vend

❖ Nous vendons

❖ Vous vendez

❖ Ils/elles vendent

5. Liaisons Guidelines

M. Dupont : J'ai envie d'acheter une nouvelle voiture.

Le collègue : Pourquoi ?

M. Dupont : Parce que ma voiture est trop vieille. Je dois la changer.

Le collègue : Est-ce que tu as une_idée de ce que tu veux acheter ?

M. Dupont : Oui. J'aimerais acheter la nouvelle Renault. Elle est superbe.

Le collègue : Oui, mais_elle doit coûter cher, n'est-ce pas ?.

M. Dupont : En effet elle coûte cher, mais_elle est moins cher que la nouvelle Peugeot et je la trouve plus belle.

Le collègue : Combien consomme-t-elle ?

M. Dupont : Sept litres au cent. Ce n'est pas beaucoup. C'est beaucoup moins que ma voiture_actuelle. En plus, elle est plus puissante.

Le collègue : Tu as raison. Tu fais une bonne_affaire.

6. Ordinal Numbers

In French, Ordinal Numbers are directly derived from the numbers by appending **ième**. There is only one exception : the French counterpart of first is not **unième** but premier.

Notes

❖ There are some irregular numbers which result in a minor alteration of the spelling (e.g. ninth is **neuvième** instead of **neufième**, fifth is **cinquième** instead of **cinqième**).

❖ 21st, 31st, 41st, etc. are translated by **vingt-et-unième**, **trente-et-unième**, **quarante-et-unième**, *etc.* and not **vingt-premier**, **trente-premier**, **quarante-premier**, *etc.* as in English.

premier	:	first
deuxième	:	second
troisième	:	third
quatrième	:	fourth

cinquième	:	fifth
sixième	:	sixth
septième	:	seventh
huitième	:	eighth
neuvième	:	ninth
dixième	:	tenth
onzième	:	eleventh
douzième	:	twelfth
treizième	:	thirteenth
quatortzième	:	fourteenth
quinzième	:	fifteenth
seizième	:	sixteenth
dix-septième	:	seventeenth
dix-huitième	:	eighteenth
dix-neuvième	:	nineteenth
vingtième	:	twentieth
vingt-et-unième	:	twenty first
centième	:	hundredth
millième	:	thousandth

The abbreviated notation of the ordinal numbers is :
1er (1st), **2ième** (2nd), **3ième** (3rd), **4ième** (4th),
21ième (21st), **31ième** (31st), **100ième** (100th),
101ième (101st), *etc.*

Lesson 9

Value for Time

$\bullet$

Let us learn the concept of time in French. Whether time is the fourth dimension of the Universe - as suggested by modern physics - or a bio-physical process which makes events irreversible, it is a reality which nobody can reject!

As a matter of fact, the way people apprehend time is strongly reflected in the human languages.

In the Western European languages (*these are the only languages I can talk about*) time is basically composed of two concepts : **the instant and the duration**.

The languages try to address these two basic concepts with an arsenal of verb tenses. Although the main principles are the same, there are sound and subtle differences between languages in the way they express time. First, let's talk about the common concepts.

Time can be thought of as a one-dimension rule where events occur. A point, or a specific position on the rule is an instant while the space between two instants is a duration. I am sure that you are very familiar with these definitions.

The time - the position on the time rule - of our conscience is the reference point : it is present time.

Before it is the past and after, the future. In the Western European languages, the basic verb tenses directly reflect this partition of time: they make provision of present, past and future tenses. However, present, past and future depict only the position - the instants - of events relative to the reference point (our conscience). Expressing the duration is subtler and varies very strongly from one language to an other one.

In this lesson, we're going to focus on the past tenses.

Vocabulary

Nouns

aujourd'hui	:	today
hier	:	yesterday
demain	:	tomorrow
un matin	:	a morning
midi	:	noon
une après-midi	:	an afternoon
un soir	:	an evening
une nuit	:	a night
le présent	:	the present
le passé	:	the past
le futur	:	the future
un jour	:	a day

une semaine	:	a week
un mois	:	a month
une année	:	a year
une heure	:	an hour
une minute	:	a minute
une seconde	:	a second

Adjectives

prochain	:	next
dernier / dernière	:	last

Conjunctions & Adverbs

tôt	:	early
tard	:	late
avant	:	before
après	:	after

Grammar

In French, there are 4 past tenses:

* l'imparfait
* le passé simple
* le passé composé
* le plus-que-parfait

The **passé** simple won't be addressed in this lesson for it is not used in the spoken language (*today, the **passé** simple is exclusively employed in literary works such as novels*).

The three other past tenses are commonly used in both the spoken and the written language.

The most popular of them is the passé composé. So, let's start with it.

1. The passé composé

The **passé composé** is the most popular but not the simpler past tense. As suggested by its name (**passé composé** means composed past), the **passé composé** is built up using an auxiliary verb.

In French, as opposed to English and Germanic languages, there are two possible auxiliary verbs : **avoir** (to have) and **être** (to be).

Basically, the **passé composé** is constructed following the pattern below:

auxiliary verb conjugated in the present tense + verb in past participle

Examples :

manger (past participle : mangé):

❖   j'**ai mangé**

❖   tu **as mangé**

❖   il/elle **a mangé**

❖   nous **avons mangé**

❖   vous **avez mangé**

❖   ils/elles **ont mangé**

aller (past participle : allé) :

❖ je **suis allé(e)**

❖ tu **es allé(e)**

❖ il/elle **est allé/allée**

❖ nous **sommes allés (es)**

❖ vous **êtes allés (es)**

❖ ils/elles **sont allés/allées**

Notes :

❖ In French, the past participle of the 1st group verbs (*verbs ending with -er*) is derived from the infinitive tense by replacing the infinitive ending (**-er**) by **-é**. This rule is always applicable ... for the 1st group verbs only!

❖ When conjugated with the auxiliary **avoir** the past participle remains unchanged whatever the subject is (**mangé** in case of the verb manger) while when the auxiliary **être** is required, the past participle changes in accordance with the gender and the number of the subject, as shown in the example above. We're going back to this remark later on.

❖ There is, unfortunately, no rule to help people determine whether a verb conjugates with the auxiliary **avoir** or **être**

There are some hints but no rigorous rule. We're going through them later on.

The Passé Composé Usage

The **passé composé** is used to express actions which took place in the past and are completed. In addition, to some extent, there may be a link, or a relationship between this past action and the present.

For instance, the past action may have consequences in the present, or the past action took place in a period which is not completed yet - though the action itself is completed - (*such a period can be an hour, a day, a week, the duration of a special event, etc.*).

In general, the **passé composé** does not bear any duration information by itself : the action may have been very long or very short.

The duration information - if required - must be added explicitly.

❖ Hier, j'ai déjeuné à 1 heure (Yesterday, I lunched at one o'clock): the lunch is now finished ! (the action of lunching is completed).

❖ L'année dernière, elle a visité le Canada (Last year, she visited Canada): the action of visiting Canada is now finished.

❖ L'avion est arrivé à 11 heures (The airplane has arrived at 11 o'clock): the airplane is now arrived (the action of arriving is completed).

❖ Hier, j'ai mangé avec mon meilleur ami (Yesterday, I ate with my best friend): the action of eating is now completed.

❖ J'ai attendu le bus pendant vingt minutes (I've waited for the bus for twenty minutes): the action of waiting is now completed.

❖ Ce matin, j'ai lu un livre (This morning, I read a book) : the book is now read (the action of reading is completed) and, in addition, the period of time (the current day in this example) is not completed.

❖ J'ai apprécié ton cadeau (I have appreciated your present) : the action of appreciating is completed but the resulting feeling (good appreciation) is still alive in the present time.

The Past Participle in French

Basically, past participle is fairly simple in French but there are lots of irregular verbs which make it more complicated than it seems at the first look. Remember the 3rd lesson dedicated to verbs: there are three verb groups in French.

❖ The 1st group: verbs ending with **-er** (aller, parler, manger, chanter, *etc.*),

❖ The 2nd group: verbs ending with **-ir** (finir, courrir, bâtir, *etc.*),

❖ The 3rd group: verbs ending with **-re** (vendre, boire, rire, *etc.*)

The past participle for the 1st verb group is built by replacing the infinitive ending by **-é**. *e.g.*:

Infinitive	Past Participle
manger (to eat)	mangé
chanter (to sing)	chanté
aller (to go)	allé
jouer (to play)	joué

The past participle for the 2nd verb group is built by replacing the infinitive ending by **-i**. *e.g.*:

Infinitive	Past Participle
finir (to finish)	fini
grandir (to grow)	grandi
choisir (to choose)	choisi
sortir (to go out)	sorti
partir (to leave)	parti

But there some major exceptions such as:

Infinitive	Past Participle
courir (to run)	couru
couvrir (to cover)	couvert

The 3rd group verbs are strongly irregular. However, in many cases, the past participle is obtained by replacing the infinitive ending by **-u**. *e.g.*:

Infinitive	Past Participle
vendre (to sell)	vendu
boire (to drink)	bu
prendre (to take)	pris
voire (to see)	vu
entendre (to hear)	entendu
vivre (to live)	vécu
mettre (to put)	mis

The **Past Participles** for the verbs **être** and **avoir** are:

être (to be)	:	été (been)
avoir (to have)	:	eu (had)

The Past Participle Concordance rules

The past participle concordance rules are certainly one of the most complicated aspects of the written French. There are two basic rules:

❖ The concordance rule for the verbs which conjugate with the auxiliary **être**

❖ The concordance rule for the verbs which conjugate with the auxiliary **avoir**

Let's start with the simpler one :

Concordance rule for the verbs which conjugate with the auxiliary être

Rule : the past participle of the verbs which conjugate with the auxiliary **être** is in concordance with the gender and the number of the subject of the verb. The concordance complies with the adjective concordance rules (the feminine is formed by appending a **-e** and the plural by appending a **-s**). *e.g.*:

❖ Ils sont allés en Amérique l'année dernière (They went to America last year): " ils " is masculine plural.

❖ Elle est arrivée en retard à l'école (literally: she arrived late at school. She was late at school): "Elle" is feminine.

❖ Le camion et la voiture sont arrivés à l'heure (the truck and the car arrived on time) : there are two items (the truck and the car) so that the subject is plural. One of the item is masculine (le camion) then the concordance rule applied is the macho rule (the masculine wins over the feminine).

Concordance rule for the verbs which conjugate with the auxiliary avoir

Rule: the past participle of the verbs which conjugate with the auxiliary (**avoir**) is in concordance with the gender and the number of the (**complément d'objet**) if it is placed before the verb (!!!) otherwise, the past participle remains unchanged. The concordance complies with the adjective concordance rules (the feminine is formed by appending a -e and the plural by appending a -s). *e.g.*:

❖   Elle a mangé des oranges (She has eaten oranges) : the **complément d'objet** is oranges. It is placed after the verb, so that the past participle is not in concordance with it.

❖   Les oranges qu'elle a mangées sont bonnes (The oranges she has eaten are good) : the **complément d'objet** is oranges. It is placed before the verb, so that the past participle is in concordance with the gender (orange is feminine in French) and number (oranges is plural) of the **complément d'objet**.

Determining The Right Auxiliary

Most of the verbs conjugate in passé composé with the auxiliary avoir. However, the number of verbs which require the auxiliary être is not negligible.

There is no reliable rule to determine whether a verb conjugates with the auxiliary être or avoir. Nevertheless, there are some hints which can help you use the right auxiliary.

The verbs which conjugate with the auxiliary être are:

❖   the " **pronominal** " verbs (verbes pronominaux),

❖   the " **intransitive** " verbs (verbes intransitifs) which express a movement or a change of state

The concepts of pronominal and intransitive verbs will be discussed in detail later in this course. However, to clarify the previous rules, let's give the following definitions :

- ❖ a pronominal verb is reflexive *i.e.*, it directly applies to the subject. In English, the pronominal verbs are those which require myself, yourself, himself, herself, ourselves, themselves.

  e.g.: I wash myself, you watch yourself in the mirror, he kills himself, *etc.* In French, the pronominal verbs are distinguished by se in front of them in the infinitive form. *e.g.* se laver (to wash oneself), se regarder (to watch oneself), se tuer (to kill oneself), se promener (to walk), s'habiller (to dress), *etc.* As you see, some verbs are transitive in French and not in English.

- ❖ an intransitive verb is a verb wich does not require a complément d'objet (an accusative). Conversely, the verbs which require a complément d'objet are called transitive. *e.g.*

Transitive Verbs	Conjugation Example
manger (to eat)	*je mange un bon repas* (I am eating a good meal)
chanter (to sing)	*Je chante une chanson* (I am singing a song)
boire (to drink)	*je bois un verre de vin* (I'm drinking a glass of wine)

Intransitive Verbs	Conjugation Example
aller (to go)	***je vais à l'école***
	(I'm going to school)
voler (to fly)	***l'avion vole***
	(the airplane flies)
rouler (to run)	***la voiture roule***
	(The car runs)

So, the main intransitive verbs which must be conjugated with the auxiliary être are:

aller	:	to go
arriver	:	to arrive
devenir	:	to become
entrer	:	to enter
mourrir	:	to die
naître	:	to be born
partir	:	to leave
rester	:	to stay
sortir	:	to go out, to get out
tomber	:	to fall
venir	:	to come

2. The Imparfait

The imparfait is the second most popular past tense in French. As opposed to passé composé, it is very easy to conjugate for it does not need any auxiliary verb.

The imparfait conjugation pattern is similar to the present tense one with some alterations.

Conjugation Of The 1st Group Verbs

chanter (to sing)
- ❖ je chantais
- ❖ tu chantais
- ❖ il/elle chantait
- ❖ nous chantions
- ❖ vous chantiez
- ❖ ils/elles chantaient

parler (to speak, to talk)
- ❖ je parlais
- ❖ tu parlais
- ❖ il/elle parlait
- ❖ nous parlions
- ❖ vous parliez
- ❖ ils/elles parlaient

écouter (to listen to)
- ❖ j'écoutais
- ❖ tu écoutais
- ❖ il/elle écoutait
- ❖ nous écoutions

❖ vous écoutiez

❖ ils/elles écoutaient

You can clearly see the conjugation pattern applying to the termination of the 1st group verbs.

❖ 1st person singular : **-ais**

❖ 2nd person singular : **-ais**

❖ 3rd person singular : **-ait**

❖ 1st person plural : **-ions**

❖ 2nd person plural : **-iez**

❖ 3rd person plural : **-aient**

Now, let's try " **aller** " which is irregular in present tense:

❖ j'allais

❖ tu allais

❖ il/elle allait

❖ nous allions

❖ vous alliez

❖ ils/elles allaient

In the imparfait, " **aller** " is no longer irregular.

Conjugation of the 2nd group verbs

finir (to finish)

❖ je finissais

❖ tu finissais

❖ il/elle finissait

❖ nous finissions

❖ vous finissiez

❖ ils/elles finissaient

venir (to come)

❖ je venais

❖ tu venais

❖ il/elle venait

❖ nous venions

❖ vous veniez

❖ ils/elles venaient

vouloir (to want)

❖ je voulais

❖ tu voulais

❖ il/elle voulait

❖ nous voulions

❖ vous vouliez

❖ ils/elles voulaient

Once again, the conjugation of 2nd group verbs respects some kind of termination pattern, however, less obvious than in the 1st group.

Some of the 2nd group verbs conjugate like " finir " (termination pattern : -ssais, -ssais, -ssait, -ssions, -ssiez, -ssaient) and others, like " venir "conjugate as the 1st group verbs.

Once again, you may have noticed that the imparfait conjugation is less irregular than the present tense.

Conjugation Of The 3rd Group Verbs

boire (to drink)
- ❖ je buvais
- ❖ tu buvais
- ❖ il/elle buvait
- ❖ nous buvions
- ❖ vous buviez
- ❖ ils/elles buvaient

vendre (to sell)
- ❖ je vendais
- ❖ tu vendais
- ❖ il/elle vendait
- ❖ nous vendions
- ❖ vous vendiez
- ❖ ils/elles vendaient

vivre (to live)
- ❖ je vivais
- ❖ tu vivais
- ❖ il/elle vivait
- ❖ nous vivions

- ❖ vous viviez
- ❖ ils/elles vivaient

The 3rd group is still a mess but less than in the present tense.

They respect the same termination pattern as the 1st group verbs (-ais, -ais, -ait, -ions, -iez, -aient) but might be subject to some alteration.

However, in most cases, the alteration is very simple : the infinitive termination -re is dropped and replaced by the conjugation termination.

" être " (to be) and " avoir " (to have)

The auxiliary verbs être and avoir are as irregular in imparfait as in the present tense.

Let's take a close look at them.

être (to be)

- ❖ j'étais
- ❖ tu étais
- ❖ il/elle était
- ❖ nous étions
- ❖ vous étiez
- ❖ ils/elles étaient

avoir (to have)

❖   j'avais

❖   tu avais

❖   il/elle avait

❖   nous avions

❖   vous aviez

❖   ils/elles avaient

Imparfait Usage

Basically, the imparfait tense is used to express actions which were in progress in a past portion of time, without specifying with precision when they began and when they completed. In general, the imparfait is used when the action has taken a certain amount of time, *i.e.* it was not an instant action.

Examples:

Je marchais silencieusement dans la rue

(I was silently walking on the street)

A cette époque, je vivais pauvrement

(At this time, I was living poorly)

Most of the time, the imparfait is employed in French in place of the progressive past (progressive preterite) in English.

This rule works very well.

Time On The Clock

The common way to ask for the time in French is:

Quelle heure est-il ?

(What time is it ? literally : what hour is it)

Il est deux heures

(it is two o'clock)

As you see, French people express the time in a way similar to English people.

There are some minor differences however:

❖   For the first half hour : il est cinq heures vingt could be literally translated as it is five hours plus twenty minutes.

❖   For the second half hour : il est cinq heures moins dix could be literally translated by it is five hours minus ten minutes.

The French counterparts of quarter and half are respectively **quart** and **demi**.

To distinguish the time in the morning and in the afternoon, English people use the abbreviations a.m. (*ante meridiem*) and p.m.(*post meridiem*).

French people don't use these abbreviations. In French, the time in the morning and in the afternoon is specified by respectively adding du matin (*in the morning*) or de l'après-midi (*in the afternoon*) after the time.

Examples :

❖   trois heures du matin = 3:00 am

❖   cinq heures et demie de l'après-midi = 5:30 pm

In addition, there is a more formal way to make this distinction which works like this:

Time on the clock	French time
1:00 am	une heure
1:00 pm	treize heures
2:00 am	deux heures
2:00 pm	quatorze heures
2:15 am	deux heures quinze
2:15 pm	quatorze heures quinze
2:30 am	deux heures trente
2:30 pm	quatorze heures trente
2:45 am	deux heures quarante cinq
2:45 pm	quatorze heures quarante cinq
2:50 am	deux heures cinquante
2:50 pm	quatorze heures cinquante
12:00 am	douze heures or midi
12:00 pm	minuit

This way of expressing the time is utilised in the train stations, the airports, at work, in any sort of time-tables.

But in the day-to-day life, people prefer to say *trois heures de l'après-midi* rather than *quinze heures*.

Lesson 10

Additional French Vocabulary

Let us learn some more French vocabulary.

Nouns

le/un grand-père	:	grand father
la/une grand-mère	:	grand mother
les grands-parents	:	the grand-parents
le/un petit-fils	:	grand-son
la/une petite-fille	:	grand-daughter
le/un neveu	:	nephew
la/une nièce	:	niece
le/un cousin	:	[male] cousin
la/une cousine	:	[female] cousin
l'/un oncle	:	uncle
la/une tante	:	aunt
le/un beau-frère	:	brother-in-law
la/une belle-soeur	:	sister-in-law
le/un beau-père	:	father-in-law
la/une belle-mère	:	mother-in-law

le/un bébé	:	baby
le/un nouveau-né	:	newborn

Verbs

se nommer	:	to be called
naître	:	to be born
épouser	:	to marry
se marier	:	to marry

Adjectives and Adverbs

aîné (e)	:	elder
familial (e)	:	family
jeune	:	young
vieux (vieille)	:	old

Expressions and Idioms

le/un grand frère	:	the older brother
la/une grande sœur	:	the older sister
le/un petit frère	:	the younger brother
la/une petite sœur	:	the younger sister
le/un gamin	·	[male] kid
la/une gamine	:	[female] kid

Countries and Citizenship

Country	Citizenship
France	français (French)
Belgique (Belgium)	belge (Belgian)
Suisse (Switzerland)	suisse (Swiss)
Angleterre (England)	anglais (English)
Allemagne (Germany)	allemand (German)
Italie (Italy)	italien (Italian)
Espagne (Spain)	espagnol (Spanish)
Irlande (Ireland)	irlandais (Irish)
Russie (Russia)	russe (Russian)
États Unis d'Amérique (USA)	américain (American)
Canada (Canada)	canadien (Canadian)
Québec (Quebec)	québécois (Quebecer)
Chine (China)	chinois (Chinese)
Japon (Japan)	japonais (Japanese)
Portugal (Portugal)	portugais (Portuguese)
Pays-bas (Netherlands)	hollandais (Dutch)
Danemark (Denmark)	danois (Danish)
Norvège (Norway)	norvégien (Norwegian)
Suède (Sweden)	suédois (Swedish)
Finlande (Finland)	finlandais (Finnish)
Pologne (Poland)	polonais (Polish)
Hongrie (Hungary)	hongrois (Hungarian)
Bulgarie (Bulgaria)	bulgare (Bulgarian)
Autriche (Austria)	autrichien (Austrian)
Roumanie (Rumania)	roumain (Rumanian)
Turquie (Turkey)	turc (Turkish)

Expressions and Idioms

The following list provides you with common French expressions and idioms.
Idioms are the most difficult aspect of any language that's why it is worth learning them.

1. Day-to-day Life
faire des courses
to go shopping

arriver à l'heure
to arrive on time

2. At Work
travailler dur
to work hard

avoir du travail par-dessus la tête
to be overloaded by work

bosser
to work

se tourner les pouces
to twiddle one's thumbs

travailler à son compte
to work

profession libérale
professional

un grand travailleur
a person who works very hard

une bête de somme
a person who works very hard

un petit chef
a low level boss, also in a pejorative meaning

un cadre supérieur
a senior executive

NOTES

....
....
....
....
....
....
....
....
....
....

Lotus